Adventures in Music

Book One

Roy Bennett

CAMBRIDGE
UNIVERSITY PRESS

The orchestra

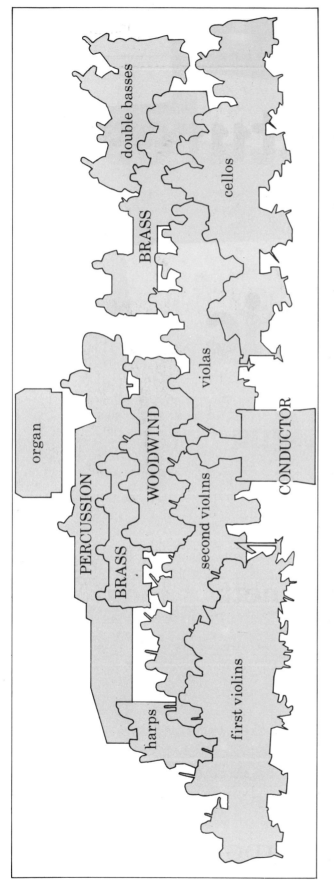

organ

PERCUSSION

BRASS

BRASS

WOODWIND

double basses

cellos

violas

second violns

first violins

harps

CONDUCTOR

Tubby the Tuba

piccolo

Tubby the Tuba introduces us to the different sections, or 'families' of instruments in the orchestra. Almost all the characters in the story are instruments. Two instruments are especially mentioned in the story – a tuba, and a piccolo.

A **tuba** is a huge brass instrument, which can make a very deep sound. A **piccolo** is a very small woodwind instrument, and the sound it makes is very high and bright.

Many other instruments also take part in the story. Listen carefully for their sounds each time the story-teller mentions their names. (You can find out more about all these instruments on the next few pages of this book.)

When the story begins, Tubby the Tuba is in a very gloomy mood. While other instruments are given interesting melodies to play, **he** is only expected to play '**oom**-pah, **oom**-pah' all the time. One evening, however, on his way home, Tubby makes a strange new friend, who teaches him to play a melody.

The next day, the famous Italian conductor, Signor Pizzicato, arrives to conduct the orchestra. Tubby takes a deep breath – and dares to play his melody. At first, the other instruments are very annoyed. Then they find that they like Tubby's melody so much, they want to join in and play it too! Here is Tubby's melody:

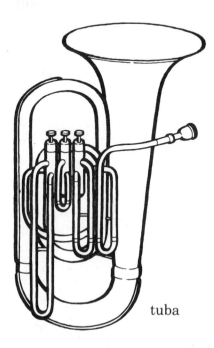

tuba

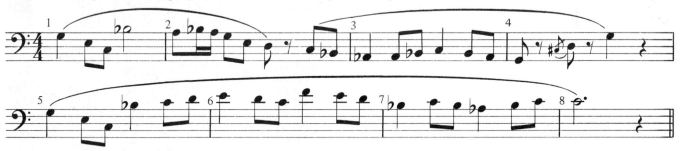

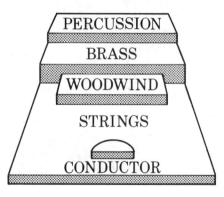

How an orchestra is put together

An orchestra is made up of four sections, or 'families' of instruments. In each of these sections, all the instruments are in some way alike. We call the four sections of the orchestra by these names:

Strings Woodwind Brass Percussion

In this drawing, you can see how the four sections of the orchestra are arranged on the concert platform.

The strings

More than half the instruments in an orchestra are string instruments.

These are: | violins   violas   cellos   double basses   harp |

Violins, violas and cellos each have four strings. Double basses sometimes have five. All these instruments make their sounds in the same way. The player presses down the strings with the fingers of the left hand, and at the same time, strokes the strings with a bow. This is a stick with horse-hair stretched along it. Sometimes the player plucks the strings with the fingertips. This is called *pizzicato*.

An important thing to remember about string instruments is this:

> The shorter the string is, the higher the sound.
> The longer the string is, the lower the sound.

Playing the violin and the cello

violin

The **violin** is the smallest of these instruments. It has the shortest strings, so it can play the highest sounds. The violin is counted as the most important instrument in the orchestra. There may be as many as 30 violins altogether. They are divided into two groups – called first violins, and second violins. The player tucks the violin under the chin when playing.

The **double bass** is so large that the player must either stand up, or perch upon a high stool. Its strings are very long and thick, and so its notes are very low. When it is played with the bow, the sound is rather 'buzzy'. But when the player plucks the strings, the sound is very rich and full.

double bass

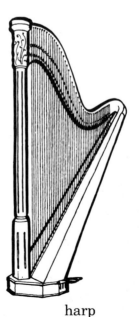

The **viola** is slightly larger than the violin. Its strings are longer, so it can play lower notes. Its sound is not as bright as the violin's but it can be very warm and rich.

viola

cello

The **cello** is about twice as large as the violin. The strings are longer and thicker and so its notes are deeper. The cello is too big to be tucked under the player's chin. Instead, it rests between the player's knees, and is propped up on the floor by a spike.

The **harp** has 47 strings. Its sounds are always made by plucking the strings with the fingertips.

The harp can play melodies. And also chords – groups of notes, which may be spread out one after another, or all played at the same moment. But the sounds you are most likely to hear from the harp are made by sweeping the fingers very swiftly across the strings.

harp

4

The woodwind

The instruments in the woodwind section of the orchestra make their sounds by being blown. This is the 'wind' part of the name *woodwind*.

All these instruments used to be made of wood. But nowadays other materials (such as metal) are used as well.

The five most important instruments in the woodwind section of the orchestra are:

flute piccolo	clarinet	oboe bassoon

Each woodwind instrument (and each brass instrument too) is a tube of some kind. When you blow, the air inside the tube vibrates to make the sound.

> A short tube will make a high sound.
> A longer tube will make a lower sound.

Playing the flute and the oboe

 flute

The **flute** is held sideways as it is played. The player blows across a hole near to one end, and makes the different notes by covering or uncovering other holes along the length of the instrument (in the same way as on a recorder).

 piccolo

The **piccolo** is really a half-sized flute. (The name *piccolo* is Italian for 'tiny'.) This instrument makes the highest, brightest sound in the whole orchestra.

The **oboe** has a *double reed* – two thin strips of cane, fastened together and fixed into the top of the instrument. As the player blows between the two reeds, they vibrate against each other. This makes the oboe sound more 'reedy' than the clarinet.

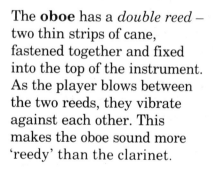 oboe

The **clarinet** has a *reed*. This is a flat piece of cane which is fixed into the mouthpiece by a metal band. The player's breath makes the reed vibrate – rather like holding a piece of grass between the thumbs and blowing. (The clarinet is not mentioned by name in *Tubby the Tuba*, but you will hear it during the middle part of the story – just before Tubby meets his new friend.)

clarinet

bassoon

The **bassoon** is the largest of these woodwind instruments, and so it makes the lowest sounds. Its very long tube is folded back on itself, to make it more easy to hold.

The bassoon has a double reed (like the oboe). This is fitted into the end of the 'crook'. It is called this because it looks like a shepherd's crook.

The brass

The brass instruments of the orchestra (like the woodwind) make their sounds by being blown. The instruments of the brass section are:

trumpet	horn	trombone	tuba

Each brass instrument is a metal tube, bent into a particular shape.

> The shorter the tube is, the higher the sound.
> The longer the tube is, the lower the sound.

A metal mouthpiece is fixed into one end of the tube. The other end of the tube widens into a 'bell'. The player presses his lips against the mouthpiece when blowing. To play a high sound, the lips are tightened . To play a lower sound, the lips are slackened.

A certain number of notes can be played just by using the lips like this. But to play other notes, the player must change the length of the tube. Let us see how this is done on the trombone.

Playing the trumpet and the horn

trombone

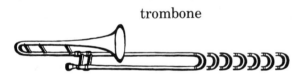

The **trombone** has a *slide*. By sliding this in and out, the player changes the length of the tube. There are seven positions for the slide. Each position gives its own set of notes. The player sounds these different notes by making the lips tighter or slacker against the mouthpiece.

 trumpet

The **trumpet** is the smallest of these brass instruments. It can play the highest notes, and also makes the brightest sound. Instead of a slide, like the trombone, the trumpet has three *valves*. When a valve is pressed down, an extra bit of tubing is added in, making the whole tube longer.

horn

The **horn** also has three valves. The player works these with the left hand, and holds the horn by resting the right hand inside the bell. The sound of the horn is usually smooth and round. But when blown hard, it can become very loud and 'brassy'.

The **tuba** is the largest instrument in the brass section of the orchestra. It·has the longest length of tube, and so it can play the lowest notes. The sound it makes is very rich and 'fat'. A tuba may have three valves, or as many as five.

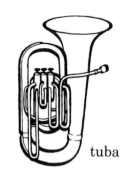

tuba

 muted trumpet

Sometimes, for a different kind of sound, a brass player fixes a *mute* into the bell of the instrument.

The percussion

On this page you can see several instruments from the percussion section of the orchestra. To make their sounds, percussion instruments are struck or shaken, clashed or banged.

The percussion instruments shown on the left, below, are able to play *musical notes*, and so they could join in playing a tune. All the instruments shown on the right may make exciting sounds – but these are *noises*, not musical notes.

Kettle drums are copper bowls with skin stretched across the top. If you tighten the skin, the note you play will be higher. If you slacken it, the note will be lower. You can make single strokes, or play a 'roll' by using both sticks alternately and very quickly. Often two or more kettle drums are used, so that more than one note can be played.

kettle drum

xylophone

The **xylophone** has bars of very hard wood. These make a strong, bright sound when they are struck with beaters.

The **glockenspiel** has strips of steel which make clear, bell-like sounds when they are hit.

glockenspiel

celesta

The **celesta** looks rather like a small piano. When keys are pressed down, tiny hammers strike steel plates, making a silvery, chiming sound.

The big **bass drum** gives out a low booming *noise* (rather than a clear *note* like the kettle drum). You may hear single 'booms' on the bass drum. Or a thunderous roll, played with kettle drum sticks.

bass drum

snare drum

The **snare drum** (sometimes called the **side drum**) has two skins. The bottom skin has lengths of catgut or wire stretched across it. These are called the snares. When the top skin is hit, the snares tremble against the bottom skin, making a rattling noise.

The **triangle** can be struck with a metal beater to make separate 'tings'. Or you may hear a *trill*, played by rattling the beater inside the top corner.

triangle

cymbals

Cymbals can be clashed together, or one cymbal may be hung up and then hit or rolled with drum sticks.

The **tambourine** is really a small drum. It has a single skin, and there are metal jingles fixed into the frame. The tambourine may be shaken, tapped, or loudly hit.

tambourine

wood block

The **wood block** is a hollow block of hard wood, tapped with a drum stick.

Tubby the Tuba

A

Name these instruments. All of them are heard during the story of *Tubby the Tuba*.

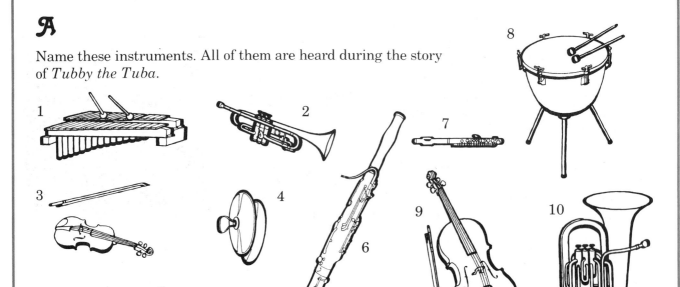

B

Draw four columns in your notebook. At the top of each column, write the name of a section of the orchestra:

Strings	Woodwind	Brass	Percussion

Now take each instrument drawn on this page and write its name in the correct column on your chart.

C

Make a drawing to show how the four sections of the orchestra are set out on the concert platform.

Colour the space taken by each section of the orchestra on your drawing. Use a different colour for each section.

D

Which instrument would **you** most like to play?
Draw the instrument you choose.
Underneath your drawing, write a sentence saying how your instrument makes its sound.

𝕃a ℝéjouissance

from 'Music for the Royal Fireworks'

George Frideric HANDEL
1685–1759
ENGLAND (born in Germany)

In spring of the year 1749, King George II of Great Britain commanded that a magnificent fireworks display should take place in Green Park in London. This was to celebrate the signing of a peace treaty, agreeing that the long war between Britain and France should now come to an end. Special music to accompany the fireworks was to be provided by the famous composer, Handel.

As the music was to be played out-of-doors, Handel decided not to include string instruments, but to use a large number of wind and percussion instruments. These sounds would carry further in the open air. So Handel's huge outdoor orchestra consisted of:

The composer of 'Music for the Royal Fireworks'

George Frideric Handel was born in 1685, in the German town of Halle. His father hoped he would become a lawyer, but Handel was very keen on music. He learned to play the violin and the harpsichord, and soon decided that he wanted to become a composer.

Handel spent most of his life outside Germany. As a young man, he travelled a great deal. He spent five years in Italy, visiting important musical towns and cities. Then he made a short visit to England.

A year later, Handel visited England again. His music was a great success, and he soon became the most famous composer in London. He decided not to return to Germany. Instead he made England his home for the rest of his life.

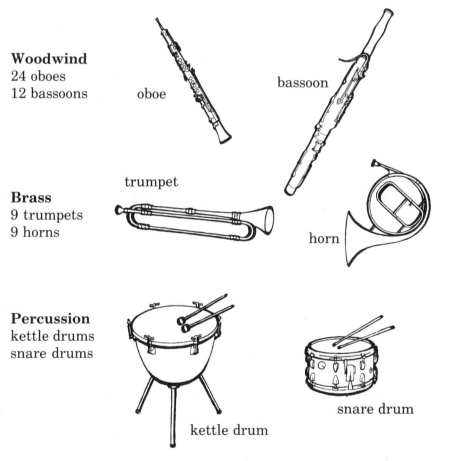

Woodwind
24 oboes
12 bassoons

oboe

bassoon

trumpet

Brass
9 trumpets
9 horns

horn

Percussion
kettle drums
snare drums

snare drum

kettle drum

As you can see, the trumpets and horns of Handel's time had no valves. Like a bugle, they could only play a limited number of notes. A player could only make these notes by changing the pressure of the lips against the mouthpiece. The higher the note, the tighter the player's lips had to be.

An enormous wooden building was put up in Green Park, with a huge gallery for all the musicians. Above the building was a model of a vast sun. This was designed to burst into flames during the fireworks display.

Thousands of people came to see the fireworks, and to hear the special music Handel had composed. First, 101 brass cannon fired a royal salute. Then Handel began to conduct his music.

One part of the music was called *La Paix*, meaning 'Peace'. Another part was called *La Réjouissance* (The Rejoicing). This was very lively music, meant to show the rejoicing of the British people at the signing of the peace treaty with France.

The enormous sun blazed gloriously above the wooden building. But the fireworks turned out to be very disappointing. Some went off in fits and starts. Others just fizzled and then went out. Some even went off in ways they were not supposed to. And as *La Réjouissance* was being played, rockets and fiery sparks showered down everywhere, frightening the crowd.

Then a terrible thing happened. One side of the huge wooden building caught fire! Everyone began to panic, pushing and jostling so that many people fell to the ground and were trampled on.

However, in spite of everything that went wrong, the music Handel composed for the royal fireworks display was a great success. Not long after, he conducted another performance of the music. This time, though, it was played indoors, and so Handel used far fewer wind instruments and included string instruments as well.

Listen to the piece called *La Réjouissance* (The Rejoicing) from Handel's 'Music for the Royal Fireworks'. The chart on the opposite page shows what happens during this piece. Follow this chart as you listen to the music.

Handel's monument in Westminster Abbey, where he was buried. It is a great honour to be buried here.

The fireworks display in Green Park, London, in 1749. Can you see the fire starting at the right-hand end of the wooden building?

La Réjouissance

1 Tune **A** – played mainly by trumpets, accompanied by the kettle drums.

trumpet

TUNE A

kettle drum

2 Tune **A** again – now played mainly by oboes, with horns and bassoons.

oboe · bassoon · horn

3 Tune **B** – mainly trumpets, with the kettle drums.

trumpet

TUNE B

kettle drum

4 Tune **B** again – mainly oboes, with horns and bassoons.

oboe · horn

5 Tune **A** – this time played by all the instruments together, and now with snare drums joining in.

snare drum

6 Tune **B** – played by all the instruments together.

11

La Réjouissance

A

Here are some of the instruments which take part in Handel's
'Music for the Royal Fireworks':

<table>
<tr><td>WOODWIND</td></tr>
<tr><td>BRASS</td></tr>
<tr><td>PERCUSSION</td></tr>
</table>

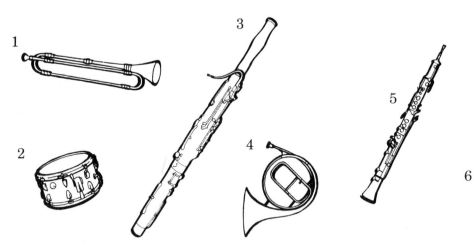

a. Name each of these instruments.
b. Match each instrument to a section of the orchestra.

B

All these words have something to do with the instruments
drawn above:

double reed		sticks
bell	mouthpiece	
skin		keys

Match each word to two different instruments.

C

Either: draw and colour a picture showing what happened at
the Royal Fireworks Display;

Or: design a poster announcing the Royal Fireworks Display in
Green Park. In your poster you could include some of the
instruments which will take part.

Alla Turca

from Piano Sonata in A major (K331)

Wolfgang Amadeus MOZART
1756–1791
AUSTRIA

This piece of music by Mozart has a rather strange title – *Alla Turca*. This means 'in Turkish style'. Although this music is played on a piano, it is meant to imitate the sound of a Turkish military band – the band of the Janissaries.

The Janissaries were the special bodyguard of the Turkish sultans. Besides being fierce soldiers, many of them were also musicians. The sounds made by the Janissary band were extremely loud. The music always had a very steady rhythm, and the first beat of each bar was made very firm and strong.

The band included trumpets, and Turkish woodwind instruments rather like flutes and oboes. But most important in the Janissary band were percussion instruments. These were

bass drums	kettle drums	cymbals	triangles

There was one other, very unusual, percussion instrument in the Janissary band. This was known as the Turkish crescent, or the 'Jingling Johnny'.

In the drawing below you can see five Janissary musicians – players from a Turkish military band. They are playing small kettle drums, cymbals, triangle, a shawm (a woodwind instrument rather like an oboe), and a bass drum.

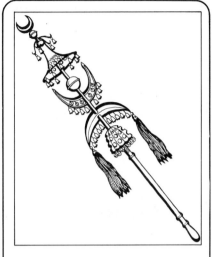

The Turkish crescent, or 'Jingling Johnny'

As you see, this was a pole with cross-bars shaped like crescents. Lots of tiny bells and jingles were hung on the instrument. And these all made bright, jingling sounds when the pole was shaken up and down, or jerked from side to side.

A 'Jingling Johnny' would be decorated with one or two shining ornaments. Sometimes horse-tail plumes of different colours were hung from it.

The bass drum has two skins – one on each side. The player uses a heavy stick on the right skin and a split rod on the left skin. He keeps the beat of the music very firm and steady:
1 2 3 4, **1** 2 3 4, **1** 2 3 4

At some time early in the 18th century, the Turkish Sultan presented the King of Poland with a magnificent gift – a complete Janissary military band! When the Empress of Russia discovered this, she was jealous and asked for a similar band to be sent to her. Before very long, music in the Turkish style was being heard all over Europe.

During the 18th century, several famous composers became interested in the sounds of the Janissary band. Sometimes they wrote pieces for orchestra in Turkish style, with noisy sounds on bass drum, cymbals and triangle.

Mozart, though, in his piece called *Alla Turca*, uses just one instrument to imitate the sounds of the Turkish Janissary band – the piano.

The composer of *Alla Turca*

Mozart was born in 1756 in Salzburg, Austria. His father taught him to play the piano when he was only four years old. A year later, Mozart was composing and playing his own pieces. While he was still a boy, Mozart travelled to most of the important cities of Europe. He gave many concerts, and often played at royal courts and palaces. Everyone was amazed at his brilliant musical gifts.

But even though he became famous, Mozart always found it difficult to earn much money. He died very poor, at the early age of 35. Only a few people bothered to attend his funeral, and no one knows exactly where he was buried.

The picture above shows part of the huge Janissary band, made up of soldier musicians chosen from the Sultan's bodyguard. You can see (from left to right) rows of trumpets, cymbals, and bass drums. At the top of the picture are kettle drum players.

Alla Turca

Follow this chart as you listen to the music.

1 First, a brisk march-tune which begins with a catchy rhythm
('**diddle-diddle-dum, diddle-diddle-dum**').

2 Then comes the main 'Turkish' tune. This music imitates the
trumpets and drums of the Janissary band.

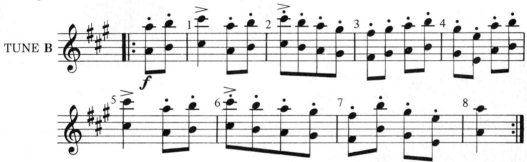

3 The third tune seems to imitate the swirling music of
high-sounding woodwind instruments.

4 Tune **B** comes round again – the 'trumpets-and-drums' tune.

5 Tune **A** is played again (the tune which begins with the
'diddle-diddle-**dum**' rhythm).

6 Tune **B** – the 'trumpets-and-drums' tune – comes round for the last time.

7 Loud music to round off the piece. Here, the piano imitates
the sounds of drums, cymbals, and jingling bells.

𝔄lla 𝔗urca

𝔄

Look at the picture of the Janissary band on page 14.

1 How many bass drums can you see?
2 How many trumpets?
3 How many cymbal players are there in the band?
4 How many kettle drum players are there?

𝔅

Several composers have written music for orchestra in 'Turkish style'. Listen to one of these pieces:

Haydn *Symphony No. 100 in G, 'The Military'* (the last minute of either the second or the fourth movement)

Mozart *Overture* to the opera 'Il Seraglio'

Beethoven *Turkish March* from the music for the play 'The Ruins of Athens'

1 As you listen to the music, make a list of the percussion instruments you hear.
2 Draw the instruments which you have listed.
3 Below each drawing, write the name of the instrument.

C

Draw your own picture of Janissary musicians playing Turkish military band instruments. Colour your picture.

𝔇

Why not make up your own 'Janissary Band'? Here is a simpler version of the main tune (the 'trumpets-and-drums' tune) from Mozart's *Alla Turca*. Listen to this tune as your teacher plays it to you.

1 Sing or whistle this tune.
   Perhaps some of you could play it on recorders or other instruments – or on comb-and-tissue-paper.

2 Use this tune to make up your own *Turkish March*. Some of you will need to play an accompaniment to the March on percussion instruments. These will make 'Turkish' sounds:

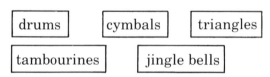

Also use any other jingling sounds you can think of – such as bunches of keys.

3 Here is another Turkish-sounding tune:

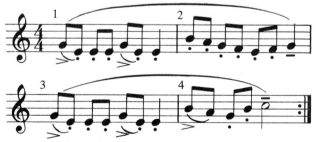

You could use this tune as well in your *Turkish March*. Or, instead, make up a Turkish-sounding tune of your own.

The Cancan

from 'Orpheus in the Underworld'

Jacques OFFENBACH
1819–1880
FRANCE (born in Germany)

Offenbach was famous for his operettas. These were comic plays in which the story was told in both speech and music. There were songs, choruses and dances, all linked together by conversations between the characters taking part.

Offenbach composed nearly 100 operettas. One of the most famous is called 'Orpheus in the Underworld'. In this operetta, Offenbach pokes fun at a very solemn Greek legend, more than 2500 years old.

The composer of the *Cancan*

Jacques Offenbach was born in Germany. But from the age of 14 he made his home in Paris, and so he is thought of as a French composer.

He first earned money as a cello player, and then as a conductor. He spent all his spare time composing music. Later, he took over a small theatre where he could conduct his own compositions.

The old Greek legend tells how Orpheus was a singer. He could also play the lyre – an instrument with strings which were plucked, like a harp.

Orpheus possessed magical powers. With his music he could charm wild animals and birds, and even plants and rocks.

The story of 'Orpheus in the Underworld', by Jacques Offenbach

In Offenbach's version of the legend, Orpheus is a violinist. He thinks very highly of himself as a musician. His wife Euridice, however, is always complaining about the noise he makes!

One day, Euridice is seized by the god Pluto, and carried off to the Underworld. ('Underworld' is a polite name for Hell.) At first, Orpheus is not too upset about his wife's disappearance! Now, perhaps, he can enjoy his music in peace. But friends soon persuade him that he really should go after his wife, and try to bring her back.

As Orpheus arrives in the Underworld, everyone – including Euridice – is having a marvellous time, dancing the Cancan. When the dance is over, Orpheus plays his violin. Everyone is so moved by his music that Pluto agrees to let Euridice go – but on one condition. Orpheus must walk ahead of his wife as they leave the Underworld, and no matter what happens he must not look back.

Orpheus begins to lead the way. Then the god Jupiter hurls a thunderbolt! This gives Orpheus such a fright that he looks round to find out what the noise can be. By looking back, of course, he breaks his promise to Pluto. Orpheus must leave the Underworld. Euridice must stay there for ever. And this seems to please everyone!

The *Cancan* music

The most famous music in Offenbach's 'Orpheus in the Underworld' is the lively, noisy, high-kicking dance called the Cancan.

Listen to the *Cancan* music from the Overture to 'Orpheus in the Underworld' by Offenbach. This is what happens in the music:

1 Introduction. Violins and woodwind instruments call and answer each other. Listen for the triangle to join in.

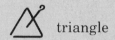 triangle

2 Then the dance begins – lightly and quietly at first, on violins.

violin

TUNE A

3 Brass instruments begin the next tune.

cymbals   trumpet

TUNE B

4 Then comes the main *Cancan* tune. This is played very loudly by the brass, with noisy sounds from percussion instruments.

trumpet   snare drum   bass drum

trombone   cymbals

TUNE C

5 The first tune (Tune **A**) is played again by the violins. Then the music grows louder, as the drums crash and roar . . .

6 . . . And we hear the exciting main tune again (Tune **C**).

7 To end the *Cancan*, the music becomes faster and noisier still! The dancers spin and whirl, until at last they flop down, breathless, upon the ground.

The Cancan

A

Here is the main tune from Offenbach's *Cancan*. Listen as
your teacher plays it to you.

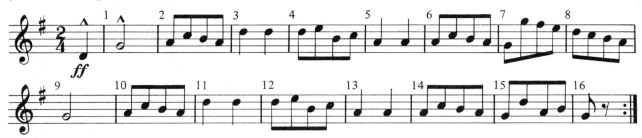

Now listen to the complete *Cancan* again.
1 Listen for the main tune. How many times is it played?
2 When you hear this tune, is it:
• always played softly?
• always played very loudly?
• played loudly at first, but softly later on?

B

The main *Cancan* tune has two very fast beats to each bar:

| one two | one two | one two | one two |

(and so on)

Listen to the *Cancan* again.
Each time the main tune comes round, clap the beats. To
keep up with the music, you will have to clap very quickly
– and very accurately!

C Crossword

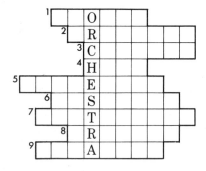

See if you can fill in the missing words using these clues:
1 The smallest string instrument in the orchestra.
2 Instead of valves, this brass instrument has a *slide*.
3 These instruments may be hit or clashed.
4 A brass instrument which is coiled round in a circle.
5 Another name for a side drum (2 words).
6 The largest drum in the orchestra (2 words).
7 This drum is a copper bowl with skin stretched tightly across
   the top (2 words).
8 A brass instrument with a high, bright sound.
9 A three-sided percussion instrument.

Music from

The Carnival of Animals

Camille SAINT-SAËNS
1835–1921
FRANCE

Saint-Saëns was very fond of animals, and wrote a book about them. One year, while he was on holiday, he composed some music which he called *The Carnival of the Animals*. Many different kinds of creature appear in this Carnival. Besides animals, there are birds, fish – and a few other, rather strange, kinds of creature as well.

The Carnival of the Animals is made up of 14 short pieces of music. You can meet seven of the creatures in the Carnival on the next few pages of this book.

The orchestra which plays the music of *The Carnival of the Animals* includes four kinds of string instrument, two woodwind instruments and four percussion instruments – a xylophone, a glockenspiel, and **two** pianos.

The composer of *The Carnival of the Animals*

Saint-Saëns was born in Paris. He became famous as a composer, and also as a very clever pianist. He first played the piano at a concert when he was only seven years old, and he was still giving concerts when he was 85.

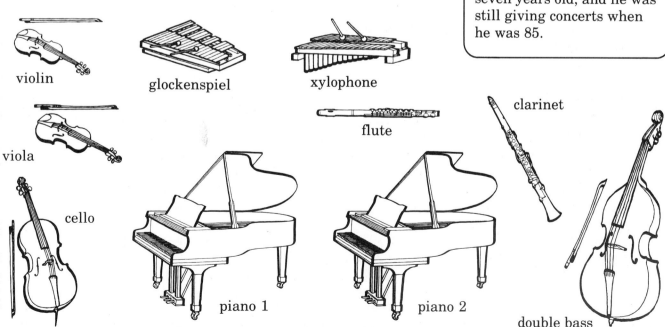

violin

glockenspiel

xylophone

viola

flute

clarinet

cello

piano 1

piano 2

double bass

Introduction, and Royal March of the Lions

1 The Lions are waking up. They yawn, and stretch, and flex their claws. (Listen to the sounds played by the string instruments.)

Suddenly, the Lions spring to their feet.

2 The two pianos play loud fanfare music.
Then we hear the tune of the *Royal March of the Lions*.

3 Loud roaring sounds, played on the pianos, warn us how fierce these creatures can be!

4 The tune of the *Royal March* is played on the pianos. Listen for more roars (now played mostly by the string instruments).

Tortoises

Very slowly, and very solemnly, the Tortoises begin to dance.

Saint-Saëns plays a musical joke here. The tune is not one he has made up himself. Instead, he borrows it from another composer mentioned in this book. Listen to the tune played in a much more lively and noisy way – and see if you can tell which tune it really is.

The Elephant

1 Here comes the Elephant, plodding along with its trunk swaying from side to side. To play the Elephant's music, Saint-Saëns chooses the huge string instrument called the double bass.

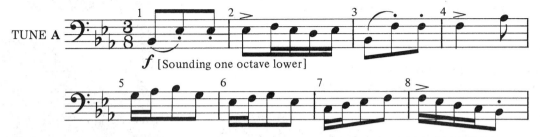

TUNE **A**

f [Sounding one octave lower]

2 It seems that this Elephant would like to be a ballet-dancer! We hear a dance-tune, which Saint-Saëns borrows from another French composer called Berlioz.

TUNE **B**

This dance-tune should sound very light and graceful. But danced by the huge Elephant, it sounds just a little bit clumsy!

3 The first tune (Tune **A**) is played again – as the Elephant goes on waltzing, very solemnly, round and round in circles.

double bass

The Aquarium

glockenspiel

Fishes of every shape and colour slowly glide through the water of the aquarium.

Listen for the cool, sparkling sounds of the glockenspiel. And for the gently falling sounds played by the pianos as, now and again, a fish spirals gracefully down through the water.

Persons with Long Ears

violin

This piece is played by just the violins. Their sounds make it quite clear which kind of long-eared creatures these are!

The Aviary

flute

This music imitates the sounds and movements of birds, chirruping and twittering as they flutter swiftly to and fro inside the aviary.

The string instruments and the two pianos help to paint this musical picture. But the most important instrument in this piece is the flute.

Fossils

This piece is another musical joke. Fossils are the remains of creatures which have been buried in the earth for thousands or even millions of years. Saint-Saëns gives the music this title because it is put together from several old tunes which he has 'dug up' from the past.

1 The first tune is played by the xylophone. Saint-Saëns borrows this tune from another piece which he had written earlier. It is the music of the skeletons' dance from his famous piece called *Danse Macabre*, meaning 'The Dance of Death'.

2 Listen for snatches of the tune *Twinkle, twinkle, little star*, played by the two pianos.

Then, just for a second or two, the clarinet plays a small part of an old French folk-song called *Au clair de la lune*, meaning 'In the moonlight':

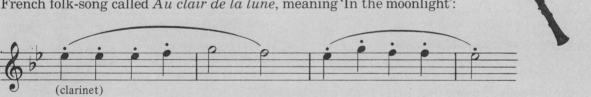

3 The tune of the skeletons' dance is played again.

4 The clarinet is given two short tunes to play. The first is a French soldiers' march. The second is part of a song from an opera by the Italian composer called Rossini.

5 Then the music of *Fossils* is rounded off by one more playing of the skeletons' dance.

25

The Carnival of Animals

A

Listen to these three tunes. Each belongs to a different creature
in *The Carnival of the Animals* by Saint-Saëns.
Can you recognise each one?

B

Which instruments are these? They all take part in
The Carnival of the Animals.

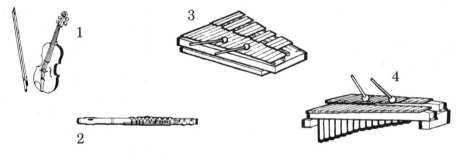

How are the sounds made on each of these instruments?

C

Design a colourful cover for a record of

> *The Carnival of the Animals*
> by Saint-Saëns

You could include drawings of some of the creatures which take
part in the Carnival – and perhaps some of the instruments
which play their music, too.

The Flight of the Bumble Bee

from the opera 'The Tale of Tsar Saltan'

Nicholas RIMSKY-KORSAKOV
1844–1908
RUSSIA

The opera tells the story of how, many years ago, in a small village in Russia, there lived three sisters. The youngest, whose name was Militrissa, was very beautiful. Her two sisters were ugly, and were often very cruel to her. One day, the mighty Tsar Saltan passed by, and saw Militrissa. He fell in love with her and took her back to his palace as his bride. He commanded her two sisters to come as well. As a punishment for their cruelty they were made servants at the palace.

The composer of *The Flight of the Bumble Bee*

Most composers find that writing music is a full-time job. But for several years, besides being a composer, Rimsky-Korsakov was also a sailor in the Russian Navy. Some of his pieces were written at sea, during the hours when he was off duty. Later, he left the navy, so that he could give all his time to music.

A year later, while the Tsar was away at war, Militrissa gave birth to a baby boy. Her two sisters quickly thought up a cruel plot to get rid of both Militrissa and her son. They sent a message to the Tsar telling him that his wife had given birth to a monster. The Tsar, horrified by the news, commanded that Militrissa and her child should be put into a barrel, and thrown out to sea.

However, the barrel was soon safely washed up onto a deserted island, called Bujan. Then a very strange thing happened. Moment by moment, Militrissa's son was quickly growing into a sturdy young Prince! He made a bow and arrow, and shot a hawk which he saw attacking a swan. The dead hawk was an evil magician, and the swan was a princess upon whom he had cast a spell. The Swan Princess, too, had magical powers. She promised the Prince that she would use her magic if ever he needed her help.

When he killed the hawk, the Prince also broke another spell. A magnificent city, which the magician had caused to vanish, now reappeared on the island. Citizens, soldiers and courtiers poured from the gates, offering the Prince a crown, and begging him to become their ruler.

After a few years, the Prince decided to visit his father, the Tsar, in secret. The Swan Princess, by her magic, changed him into a bumble bee, and in this disguise he left Bujan.

At the palace, the Tsar was entertaining the captain of a ship which had just arrived from Bujan. When the Tsar heard what a wonderful place it was, he decided that he must visit Bujan immediately. Militrissa's sisters (who were now important ladies of the court) tried to prevent this. They had heard that the Prince of Bujan had a beautiful mother, and they feared the Tsar might fall in love with her and bring her back to the palace.

But the Prince, in his disguise as a bumble bee, zoomed swiftly down and began to buzz furiously around all the courtiers. He stung first one sister, and then the other! They both ran shrieking out of the room – leaving the Tsar to make his plans to visit Bujan.

Next day, the Tsar and his court set sail for Bujan. They were received with great ceremony by the Prince and his mother. Of course, as soon as the Tsar saw Militrissa, he fell in love with her again. As for the Prince, he made the lovely Swan Princess his bride. And they ruled Bujan together for many years.

The Flight of the Bumble Bee

This is one of Rimsky-Korsakov's most famous pieces. It is very short, and the music is extremely fast! The picture-chart below shows the zooming, buzzing flight of the bumble bee. See if you can follow the chart as you listen to the music.

As you can see, the flight has been timed. These timings match a recording of the music which lasts 1 minute 34 seconds – but some orchestras play this piece faster than others.

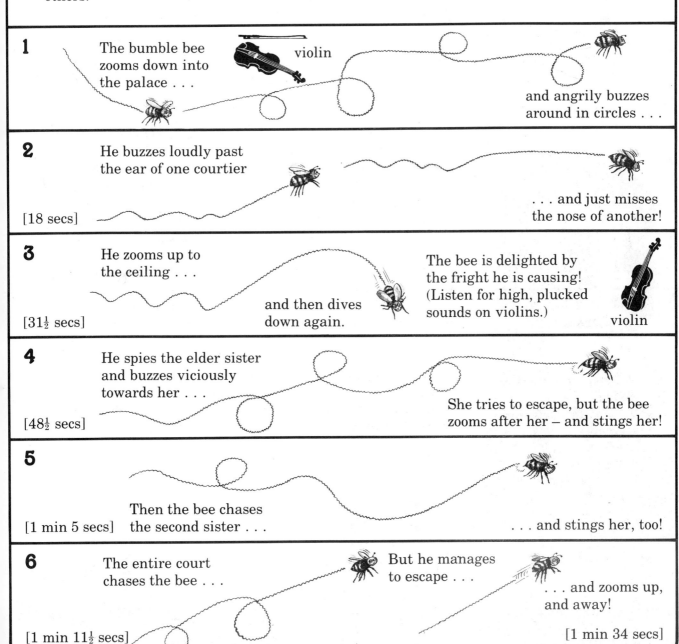

1 The bumble bee zooms down into the palace . . .

violin

and angrily buzzes around in circles . . .

2 He buzzes loudly past the ear of one courtier

[18 secs]

. . . and just misses the nose of another!

3 He zooms up to the ceiling . . .

and then dives down again.

The bee is delighted by the fright he is causing! (Listen for high, plucked sounds on violins.)

violin

[31½ secs]

4 He spies the elder sister and buzzes viciously towards her . . .

[48½ secs]

She tries to escape, but the bee zooms after her – and stings her!

5 Then the bee chases the second sister . . .

[1 min 5 secs]

. . . and stings her, too!

6 The entire court chases the bee . . .

But he manages to escape . . .

. . . and zooms up, and away!

[1 min 11½ secs]

[1 min 34 secs]

29

The Flight of the Bumble Bee

𝔄 Crossword

Fill in the missing words of this crossword by using these clues:

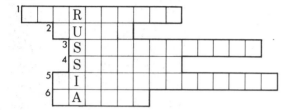

1 He commanded that Militrissa and her baby should be cast out to sea in a barrel. (2 words)
2 The barrel was safely washed up on the Island of . . . . .
3 The Prince was turned into a bumble bee by the magic of the . . . . (2 words)
4 The bumble bee chased and stung the two . . . .
5 The composer of *The Flight of the Bumble Bee*.
6 Besides being a composer, he was also a . . . . . .

𝔅

Here are the names of the four kinds of string instrument which play *The Flight of the Bumble Bee* from Rimsky-Korsakov's opera 'The Tale of Tsar Saltan'

1 Which of these string instruments plays the *highest* sounds?
2 Which plays the *lowest* sounds?
3 Which two of these instruments are tucked under the chin as they are being played?
4 Which of them is propped up on the floor by a spike?

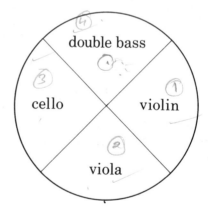

C

Sometimes *The Flight of the Bumble Bee* is played in a special version featuring a single instrument. For instance:

piano	harpsichord	flute	clarinet	trumpet	cello

1 Listen to one of these special performances.
2 Listen again, and time the performance. How long does the performer take to play the music?

The Ritual Fire Dance

Manuel de FALLA
1876–1946
SPAIN

The Ritual Fire Dance is the most exciting part of a ballet called 'Love, the Magician'. The music for this ballet was written by a Spanish composer called Manuel de Falla.

A ballet is a story which is set to music, and then danced. Usually, when someone tells you a story, they use words to tell you what happens. But in a ballet, no words are spoken at all. Instead, the story is told through the dancing, and the music.

Falla's ballet called 'Love, the Magician' takes place in Spain. It tells a story about Spanish gypsy folk. It is also about a ghost!

The composer of *The Ritual Fire Dance*

Falla's ballet tells the story of a beautiful young gypsy girl called Candélas. Her husband has recently died. But Candélas is far from unhappy about this, since he was often very cruel to her. Besides, she has now fallen in love with a handsome young gypsy named Carmelo. Unfortunately, each time the lovers meet, Candélas is haunted by the jealous ghost of her dead husband.

Candélas and Carmelo decide upon a plan. They will try to get rid of the ghost by means of witchcraft and magic. Midnight will be the best time. And all their gypsy friends must help them. This is what will happen:

At midnight, all the gypsies must make a large circle around the fire which burns in the centre of the gypsy camp. Inside this circle, Candélas will perform the mysterious Ritual Fire Dance. This will cause the ghost to appear, and then she will make him dance with her. Faster and faster they will whirl, round and round the fire – until, by the magic of the Ritual Fire Dance, he will be drawn into the flames, and vanish for ever . . .

Falla was born in the town of Cadiz, on the southern coast of Spain. This part of Spain is called Andalusia. Many years ago, gypsies settled there after travelling great distances from central Europe. This is why the folk music of Andalusia often has the colourful sounds of Spanish gypsy music.

Falla became very interested in this folk music. Sometimes in his compositions, he used the exciting rhythms of Spanish songs and dances. But he usually made up all the tunes himself.

The Ritual Fire Dance

Follow the chart as you listen to this piece of music.

1 First – mysterious buzzing sounds, which rise and fall.
Then the swaying rhythm of the Ritual Fire Dance begins.

2 The dance begins to weave its magic. The first tune is played
by an oboe. Then it is played again by the violins.

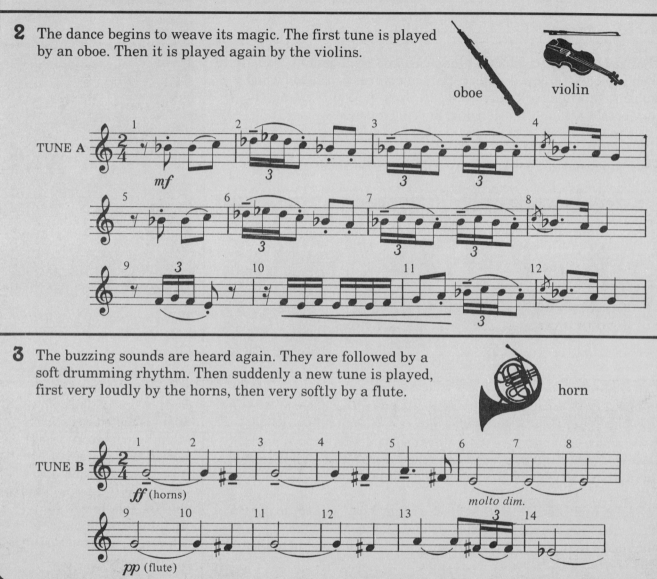

oboe   violin

TUNE A

3 The buzzing sounds are heard again. They are followed by a
soft drumming rhythm. Then suddenly a new tune is played,
first very loudly by the horns, then very softly by a flute.

horn

TUNE B

ff (horns)

molto dim.

pp (flute)

4 The third tune is played by violins, with a rhythm crashed out on the kettle drums.

violin

kettle drum

TUNE C

5 Listen for the mysterious buzzing sounds again. They are followed by Tune **A** – first on the oboe, then on the violins.

oboe   violin

6 More buzzing sounds – followed by the soft drumming rhythm. Then Tune **B** again, very loudly, on the horns.

horn

7 The third tune (Tune **C**) comes round again, as the two dancers whirl even faster around the fire.

8 Listen for wild music played by muted trumpets, as the ghost is drawn nearer and nearer to the flames . . .

Then *The Ritual Fire Dance* ends with loud chords, crashed out by the whole orchestra.

muted trumpet

The Ritual Fire Dance

A

Listen to the beginning of the music of *The Ritual Fire Dance*.
As you listen, answer these questions:

1 Does the music begin softly, or loudly?
2 The first tune is played by an oboe. Which instruments play
it next?
3 How can you tell from the music when the ghost suddenly
appears?

B

Which instruments are these? Each of them plays an important
part in the music of *The Ritual Fire Dance*.

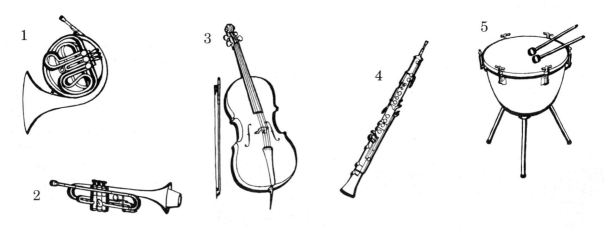

a. Which of these instruments belongs to the strings section of
the orchestra?
b. Which of them is a percussion instrument?
c. Which **two** instruments belong to the same section of the
orchestra? Which section is it?
d. Which instrument is a woodwind instrument with a double
reed?

C

Draw and colour a picture, showing what happens during the
scene in Falla's ballet when *The Ritual Fire Dance* is played.

The Viennese Musical Clock

from the opera 'Háry János'

Zoltán KODÁLY
1882–1967
HUNGARY

This music is from an opera about a Hungarian soldier called Háry János. We would call him John Háry, but in Hungary, the custom is to put the christian name *after* the surname – Háry János.

When the opera begins, Háry János is already an old man. He is a great boaster. He loves to sit in the village tavern and tell stories about his adventures as a brave young soldier. These sound very exciting – but Háry János makes them all up!

First he tells everyone his story of how he came to meet the Austrian Emperor's daughter. She was being held prisoner by the Russians. Háry János rescued her, and took her safely home to her father's palace in Vienna.

Everything there was strange and magnificent. Each flower in the palace garden was of gold and shaped like a crown. The double-headed eagle on the palace roof was fed each day with two live chickens – one for each head. But the most marvellous thing of all which Háry János saw in Vienna was a huge clock. Every time this clock chimed the hour, doors opened and a procession of clockwork soldiers came strutting out to the sounds of a bright march-tune.

The composer of *The Viennese Musical Clock*

Zoltán Kodály was born in a small country town in Hungary. As a boy, Kodály sang in the church choir. With a little help, he taught himself to play the piano, violin, and cello. When he was seventeen, Kodály went to study music in Budapest, Hungary's capital city.

Kodály became very interested in Hungarian folk music. He would travel many kilometres through the countryside. When he heard a peasant singing or playing a folk tune, he would write it down. One of the first compositions which made Kodály famous was his opera called *Háry János*. Kodály used some Hungarian folk tunes in this music, but made up all the other tunes himself.

The magnificent Viennese Musical Clock

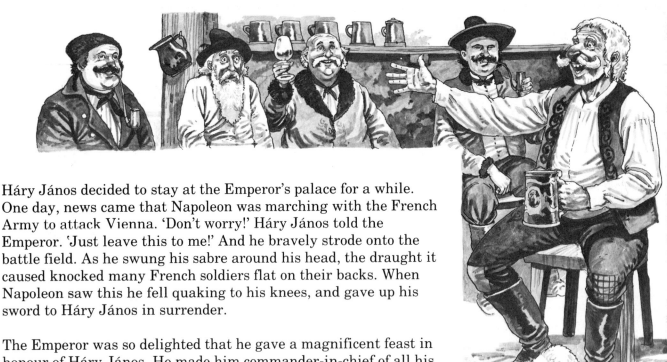

Háry János decided to stay at the Emperor's palace for a while. One day, news came that Napoleon was marching with the French Army to attack Vienna. 'Don't worry!' Háry János told the Emperor. 'Just leave this to me!' And he bravely strode onto the battle field. As he swung his sabre around his head, the draught it caused knocked many French soldiers flat on their backs. When Napoleon saw this he fell quaking to his knees, and gave up his sword to Háry János in surrender.

The Emperor was so delighted that he gave a magnificent feast in honour of Háry János. He made him commander-in-chief of all his armies, and offered him half of his kingdom. But Háry János decided he would rather return to his village in Hungary. 'After all,' he tells his listeners sitting round him in the tavern, 'if I hadn't refused the Emperor's offer, I wouldn't be sitting here telling you all this!'

The Viennese Musical Clock

Listen to Kodály's piece and follow the chart to see what happens during the music:

1 The clock begins to strike the hour. Whirring and chiming sounds are heard.

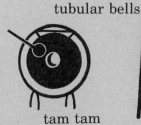

snare drum

tam tam

tubular bells

2 The clockwork soldiers begin to march round.

piccolo

glockenspiel

TUNE A

ff

3 A new tune – for trumpet and piccolo.

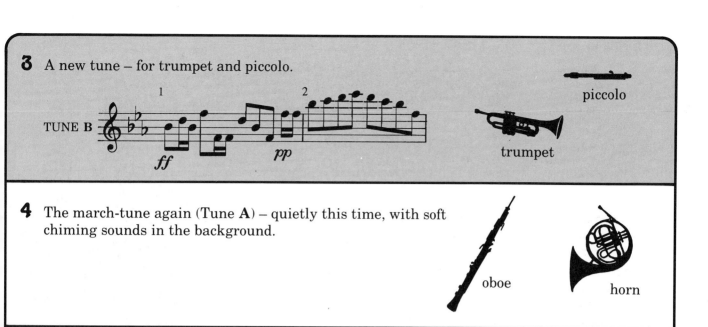

TUNE B

ff   *pp*

piccolo

trumpet

4 The march-tune again (Tune **A**) – quietly this time, with soft chiming sounds in the background.

oboe

horn

5 A tune for woodwind instruments, with cymbals, triangle, and snare drum.

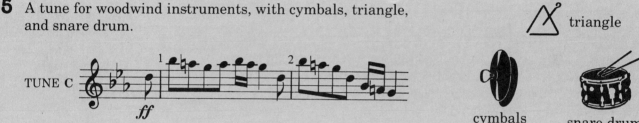

TUNE C

ff

triangle

cymbals

snare drum

6 The march-tune again (Tune **A**) – high on a flute.

flute

7 Another tune – first oboes, then trumpets.

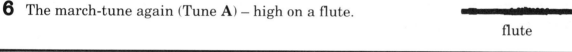

TUNE D

ff   3   3

oboe

trumpet

8 The march-tune for the last time – played loudly on a trumpet.

trumpet

9 Exciting fanfares, as the soldiers march back inside the clock and disappear.

MARINO INSTITUTE OF EDUCATIO.

The Viennese Musical Clock

A

We divide the orchestra into four sections of instruments.
The instruments in each section are alike in some way.
We call the four sections of the orchestra by these names:

Woodwind	Brass	Strings	Percussion

Only *three* of the four sections of the orchestra take part in
Kodály's piece called *The Viennese Musical Clock*.

1 Draw three boxes, like this:

2 Listen to the music. In your boxes, write the names of the
three sections of the orchestra which you hear.

3 Which section of the orchestra does *not* take part in this
music?

B

Look at this chart.

Woodwind	....	....
....	....	tubular bells
....	horn	....
....		....
clarinet		....
		....
		....

The names of three instruments are already filled in.
And the name of one section of the orchestra.

Listen to *The Viennese Musical Clock* again. See how many
missing words you can fill in.

C Crossword

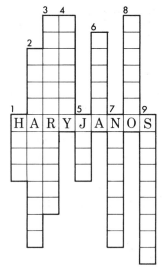

Use these clues to
fill in the missing words:

1 An instrument from the
  brass section of the
  orchestra.
2 The name of the
  composer of *The Viennese
  Musical Clock* (2 words).
3 This very large
  percussion instrument
  imitates the sound of
  bells (2 words).
4 The country where
  Kodály was born.
5 János is the same as the
  English name . . . .
6 The Emperor's palace
  was in the city of . . . . . .
7 This famous French
  general surrendered to
  Háry János.
8 A tiny woodwind
  instrument with a very
  high sound.
9 This kind of drum makes
  a bright rattling sound
  (2 words).

Things to do

𝕯

Here is the march-tune from *The Viennese Musical Clock*:

1 Sing or whistle this tune. Perhaps some of you could play it on recorders, or on other instruments.

2 Make up an accompaniment on percussion instruments, or with hand-claps. Here are some rhythms to try:

a)    b)

3 Those of you singing or playing the tune could try it as a **round** (like *Frère Jacques*, or *London's Burning*).

   Divide into two groups.
   Group 1 starts off with the tune.
   As soon as they have sung four notes, Group 2 begins the tune.

4 Some of you could play a **'background'** on glockenspiels, to imitate the chiming of the clock.

   Play the first four notes of the tune, over and over again, right through the piece.

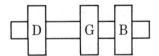   

𝕰

Either: draw and colour your own picture of the magnificent Viennese Musical Clock.

Or: imagine that you are Háry János with your friends in the tavern. Tell about one of your amazing adventures as a brave young Hungarian soldier.

March: 'The Dam Busters'

Eric COATES
1886–1957
BRITAIN

This exciting march was written for the sound-track of a film called 'The Dam Busters'. The film tells the story of 617 Squadron of the Royal Air Force.

During the Second World War, it became necessary for Britain to destroy three huge dams in the Ruhr valleys of West Germany. These dams supplied both water and electric power for many factories which were making important parts for German tanks, trains, guns and aircraft.

617 Squadron, a Lancaster bomber force, was specially formed to carry out the task of bombing the dams. The leader of this bomber force was Wing Commander Guy Gibson. And the men under his command became known as 'The Dam Busters'.

The composer of the March, *The Dam Busters*

When he was a boy, Eric Coates learned to play the violin and the viola. He formed a family orchestra, and invited other musicians who lived nearby to join in as well.

He went to London to study music, and later became a viola player in an orchestra. But his main interest was in writing music. All his pieces are 'light' and tuneful, and use the sounds of the orchestra in a very exciting way.

Eric Coates composed his *March* for the film 'The Dam Busters' in 1955. The mood of the music expresses the courage of the men of 617 squadron – and of their leader, Wing Commander Guy Gibson.

In this scene from the film of 'The Dam Busters', Wing Commander Guy Gibson looks back at the broken dam.

The first thing to be done was to work out a careful plan of how the dams were to be destroyed. Special bombs called 'bouncing bombs' were invented. When they were dropped from the aircraft they would bounce along on the surface of the water, in the same way as when you skim a pebble across a lake. They would hit the wall of the dam, but they would not explode until they had sunk deep into the water against the wall. This would make the force of the explosion much greater.

Guy Gibson realised that two things were very important – the exact speed at which the aircraft flew towards the dam, and the exact height of the aircraft above the water.

One evening, Guy Gibson went to the cinema. During the interval he noticed two spotlights, one on each side of the cinema, shining onto the closed curtains. The spotlights were angled in such a way that their beams met at precisely the same point on the curtains.

The spotlights gave Guy Gibson an idea. He worked out a clever way of knowing exactly when an aircraft had flown down to reach the correct height above the water. Each bomber was fitted with two tiny spotlights. They shone down, and inwards, beneath the plane. When the beams pinpointed down and *met* on the surface of the water, then the plane was flying at precisely the right height for the bombs to be released.

March: 'The Dam Busters'

Follow the chart as you listen to the music.
There are two very different tunes in this march. The second
tune, which is very song-like, is heard three times altogether.

1 Introduction. Music which climbs higher and higher –
building up excitement.

kettle drum

cymbals

snare drum

2 A brisk march-tune begins, played mainly by the clarinets.
(Listen, too, for triangle and glockenspiel.)

triangle

glockenspiel

clarinet

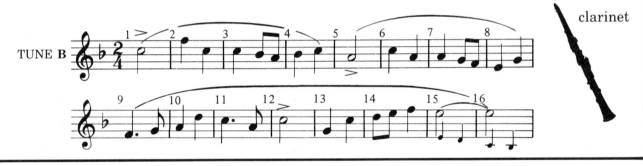

TUNE A

3 Then a new tune – smoother and more song-like.

clarinet

TUNE B

4 The second tune (Tune **B**) is played again – this time more
loudly, by trumpets and trombones.

(Above the tune, woodwinds play a high 'descant'.)

trumpet

trombone

5 The brisk march-tune (Tune **A**) is played again.

Then the music builds up excitingly . . .

triangle

glockenspiel

6 . . . And the song-like tune (Tune **B**) comes round again –
this time played more slowly, with a broad march-rhythm.

snare drum

cymbals

March: 'The Dam Busters'

A

In Eric Coate's March called *The Dam Busters*, the main tune
(Tune **B**) on page 42 is heard three times altogether.
Listen to the March again.

1 When you hear the tune played for the first time, clap each
   beat of the steady march-rhythm:

BEATS	One two	One two	One two	(and so on)
CLAP →	Ⓧ Ⓧ	Ⓧ Ⓧ	Ⓧ Ⓧ	

2 The tune is played again straight away. Clap each beat – and
   also tap your foot each time you count 'One'.

3 The tune comes round for the third time towards the end of
   the March. Clap each beat. Try singing or whistling the tune
   at the same time.

B

Eric Coates composed his March *The Dam Busters* as the theme
music for a war film. Listen to themes from other films. As you
listen to each piece see if you can tell, from the music, which
kind of film it is.

WAR?   MYSTERY?   Comedy?   SPACE?
SPY?   Love?   HORROR?
Adventure?   musical?   COWBOY?

C

1 A new record is soon to be on sale in the shops. All the pieces
   on the record will be marches of various kinds. One of them
   will be *The Dam Busters*. Name some other marches which
   you think could be played on this record.

2 Draw and colour a picture which could be used on the cover
   of this record.

Sleigh Ride and The Typewriter

Leroy ANDERSON
1908–1975
AMERICA

Almost all Leroy Anderson's pieces are 'pictures in music'. Here are the names of some of his pieces:

Sleigh Ride
The Typewriter
The Waltzing Cat
Buglers' Holiday
The Syncopated Clock
The Phantom Regiment

Leroy Anderson's pieces are full of good tunes and very catchy rhythms. He uses the sounds of the orchestra in a very vivid way. Sometimes he includes other sounds as well. (In one piece, you will hear the sounds of a typewriter!) His music is fun to listen to, and great fun to play. Orchestras always enjoy playing his pieces.

The composer of *Sleigh Ride* and *The Typewriter*

Leroy Anderson was born in Massachusetts in the United States of America. He studied music at a famous university in America called Harvard. Besides learning how to compose music, he also learned to play the organ and the double bass. Sometimes he conducted the University Band.

A few years ago, one of Leroy Anderson's pieces called *Blue Tango* reached number one in the pop music charts. It was the first time an orchestral piece, rather than a song, became 'top of the pops'.

Sleigh Ride

The music describes a brisk ride through the snow in a horse-drawn sleigh. This is what happens during this lively and joyful piece. Follow the chart as you listen.

1 Introduction. Trumpet fanfares, and the bright jingling of sleigh bells as the horses set off at a lively trot.

 trumpet

 sleigh bells

2 Violins play the main tune:

TUNE A

 violin

sleigh bells

wood block

Later, listen for wood blocks, imitating the clip-clop of the horses' hooves.

3 Tune **A** is played again, this time with brass instruments joining in.

 trumpet

 sleigh bells

4 A new tune is heard:

TUNE B

Listen for sleigh bells and wood blocks.

 sleigh bells

wood block

5 Listen for Tune **A,** played by the trumpets in a very joyful, 'jazzed-up' way.

Then violins take over the tune.

 trumpet

sleigh bells

 violin

wood block

6 Tune **A** is played for the last time.

 trumpet

 sleigh bells

7 Listen for the horses to be brought to a halt as the sleigh ride comes to an end.

 sleigh bells

45

The Typewriter

Look at the picture of the typewriter. You probably know that to type a word on the paper, you find the *keys* with the right letters on them, and press them down one by one. (Can you find the keys you would need to type out the letters of your name?)

When you type a line of words onto the paper, the *carriage* moves to the left, a little at a time. As you get to the end of the line, a *bell* tings. You must push the *lever* to make the carriage slide across to the right again. This also moves the paper up, so that you can type your next line lower down the page.

carriage

key

lever –
(push to the right at the end of a line when the bell tings)

The Typewriter

In this music you will hear many of the instruments of the orchestra, but the most important 'instrument' in this piece is — a typewriter!

1 Swift, scurrying music – as the typist quickly winds a sheet of paper into the typewriter.

2 The typist sets to work, swiftly tapping the keys.

When the bell tings, the typist pushes the lever – then rushes on, typing the next line down the page.

3 Work slows down . . . For a while, the typist taps out the letters in a slower rhythm.

4 Suddenly fast again! The typist's fingers fly over the keys in a mad dash to type to the bottom of the page.

Sleigh Ride and The Typewriter

A

Listen again to Leroy Anderson's piece called *Sleigh Ride*.

1 You hear certain instruments which tell you that this music is about a ride through the snow in a horse-drawn sleigh. Which instruments are they?
2 How does each of these instruments make its sound?
3 Make drawings of these instruments.

B

Here are four instruments you hear during *Sleigh Ride* – but the letters in each name have got mixed up. Which instruments are they?

PETTRUM	NILVIO	DOWO CKLOB

SHIGEL SLEBL

C

Listen to the beginning of *The Typewriter* by Leroy Anderson. Pretend that **you** are the typist as you listen.

- Use the fingers of both hands to tap out the letters.
- Each time you hear the 'ting' of the bell, quickly work the lever with your left hand – then go on typing along the next line of your page.

D

Listen to some other music by Leroy Anderson. You will especially enjoy his pieces called *The Syncopated Clock* and *The Waltzing Cat*.

E

A new record of music by Leroy Anderson will soon be on sale in the shops. The first piece on the record will be *Sleigh Ride*. Draw and colour a picture which could be used on the cover of this record. (You could also include drawings of other pieces by Leroy Anderson which you have heard.)

F Crossword

Fill in the missing letters in the crossword to make the names of 11 instruments.

These drawings are the clues to the crossword:

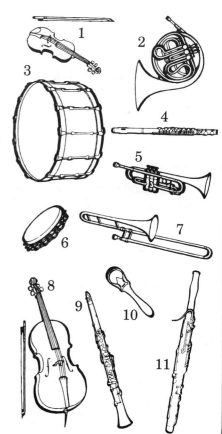

The instruments of the orchestra

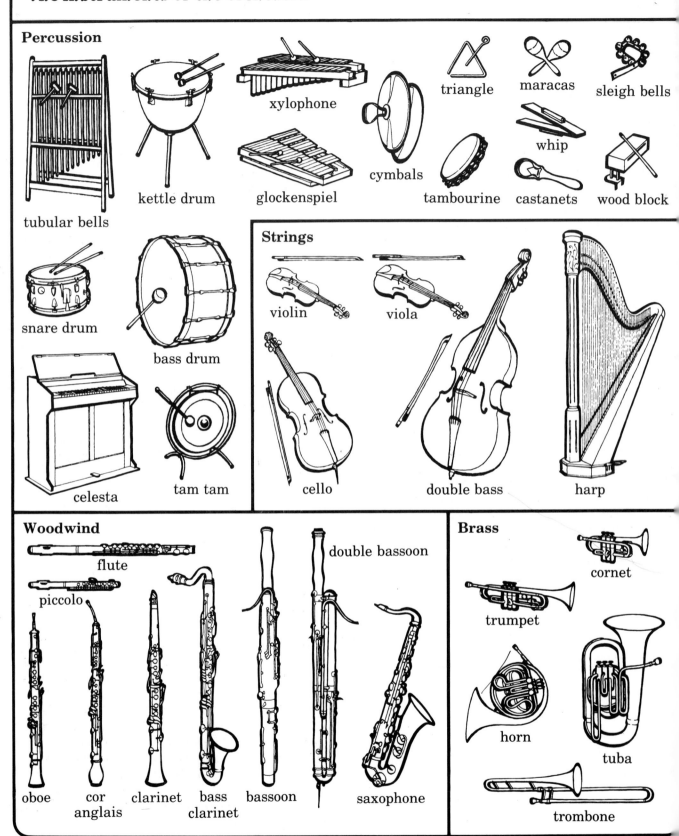

Percussion

tubular bells

kettle drum

xylophone

glockenspiel

cymbals

triangle

maracas

sleigh bells

whip

tambourine

castanets

wood block

snare drum

bass drum

celesta

tam tam

Strings

violin

viola

cello

double bass

harp

Woodwind

flute

piccolo

double bassoon

oboe

cor anglais

clarinet

bass clarinet

bassoon

saxophone

Brass

cornet

trumpet

horn

tuba

trombone